BOOK 2

MASTER YOUR SPELLING

Geoff Davies
Sue Dillon
Terry Dillon

SIMON & SCHUSTER
EDUCATION

First edition published in 1983 by
Basil Blackwell Ltd

Second edition published in 1993 by
Simon & Schuster Education
Campus 400
Maylands Avenue
Hemel Hempstead
Herts HP2 7EZ

Reprinted in 1994

A catalogue record of this book is available from the British Library.

ISBN 0 7501 0528 3

Design and typesetting by Can Do Design
Illustrated by Roger Backwell
Printed in Great Britain by Redwood Books, Trowbridge

Contents

How to Master your Spelling

To learn the words in this book:

do the activities.

Then, *for* each word you don't already know well:

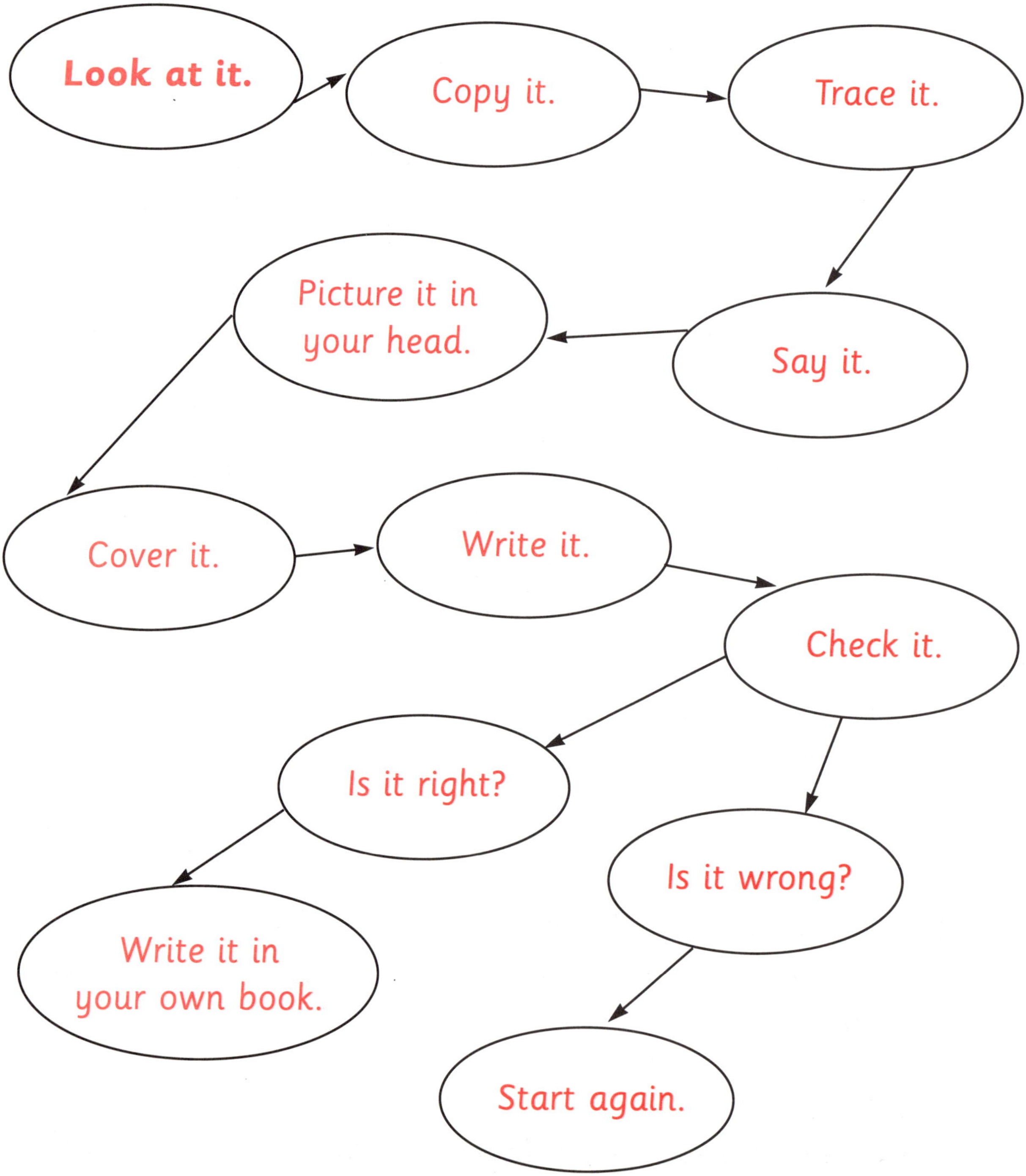

An elephant never forgets

bone box chair Christmas drinking holly north room snake stay

1 Copy the sentences below into your book. Fill in the missing words.

a Laura had a new bike for C _ _ _ _ _ _ _ s.
b The visitor gave Gran a b _ x of chocolates.
c Louise fell off her c _ _ _ r.
d There was a cold n _ _ _ h wind blowing.
e The boy fell over and broke a b _ _ e in his foot.
f Jenny's r _ _ m had a new carpet.
g A grass s _ _ _ e is not dangerous.
h Rosie went to s _ _ _ at her Gran's house.
i Nick is d _ _ _ k _ _ _ his can of orange juice.
j Mind those prickly leaves on the h _ _ l _ bush!

2 Use the picture clues to complete the sentences below.

a Nayan was too excited to go to s _ _ _ p.
b The t _ _ _ h _ _ marked our work.
c Gemma has a new r _ d umbrella.
d Look at the c _ _ c _ and tell me the time, please.
e When the b _ _ l rings we go out to play.
f Sarah likes to go h _ _ s _ riding.

Short a and e

1 Use the words in the box to help you answer the clues below. Write the words in your book.

act	**alphabet**	**ant**	**antelope**
apple	**atlas**	**attic**	**awake**

a not asleep a _ _ _ _
b a fruit a _ _ _ _
c a to z a _ _ _ _ _ _ _
d a type of deer a _ _ _ _ _ _ _
e book of maps a _ _ _ _
f room at the top of a house a _ _ _ _
g tiny insect a _ _
h in a play a _ _

2 Use the words in the box to complete the sentences below. Write them in your book.

edge	**egg**	**elbow**	**elephant**
empty	**ever**	**every**	

a The king and queen lived happily e _ _ _ after.
b We had e _ _ and bacon for breakfast.
c Matthew cut his head on the e _ _ _ of the step.
d The huge e _ _ _ _ _ _ _ walked through the jungle.
e The sweet jar is e _ _ _ _ .
f Helen got e _ _ _ _ sum right.
g The boy fell and grazed his e _ _ _ _ .

o and oi

1 Solve the picture clues below.
Write the words in your book.

a g _ _ _ _ **b** m _ _ _ _

c s _ _ **d** m _ _ _ _ _

come	**done**	**glove**	**money**	**monkey**
	oven	**son**	**won**	

2 Use the words in the box to complete the sentences below.

a Would you like to c _ _ _ to my party?
b Kiran had not d _ _ _ his homework.
c Mrs Taylor cooked the pie in the o _ _ _ .
d Kenny ran fast and w _ _ the race.
e The m _ _ _ _ _ hung from the branch by its tail.

3 Use the words in the box to complete the sentences below. Write them in your book.

boil	**noisy**	**soil**	**spoil**	**voice**

a Daniel has a very loud v _ _ _ _ .
b The children were very n _ _ _ _ at the party.
c You should b _ _ _ the egg for five minutes.
d Don't s _ _ _ _ your new shoes.
e The worm burrowed into the s _ _ _ .

Months of the year

1 Roger Rabbit has got the months mixed up. Write them in your book in the correct order.

October **March** **January**
July **May** **February** **December**
April **June** **November** **September**
August

2 Use the months to complete the sentences below. Write them in your book.

a Bonfire Night is on 5th N _ _ _ _ _ _ _ _.
b New Year's Day is on 1st J _ _ _ _ _ _ _.
c Christmas Day is on 25th D _ _ _ _ _ _ _ _.
d Hallowe'en is on 31st O _ _ _ _ _ _ _ .
e The shortest month is F _ _ _ _ _ _ _ _.
f The fifth month of the year is M _ _.
g The month after June is J _ _ _.
h My birthday is in ________________.

3 Sort out the letters below to make months of the year. Write the months in your book.

a neJu
b rhMca
c petmbSeer
d iAlrp
e gtAsuu

u and ould

1 Use the words in the box to complete the sentences below. Write them in your book.

bull **bush** **full** **pudding** **pulled** **push** **sugar**

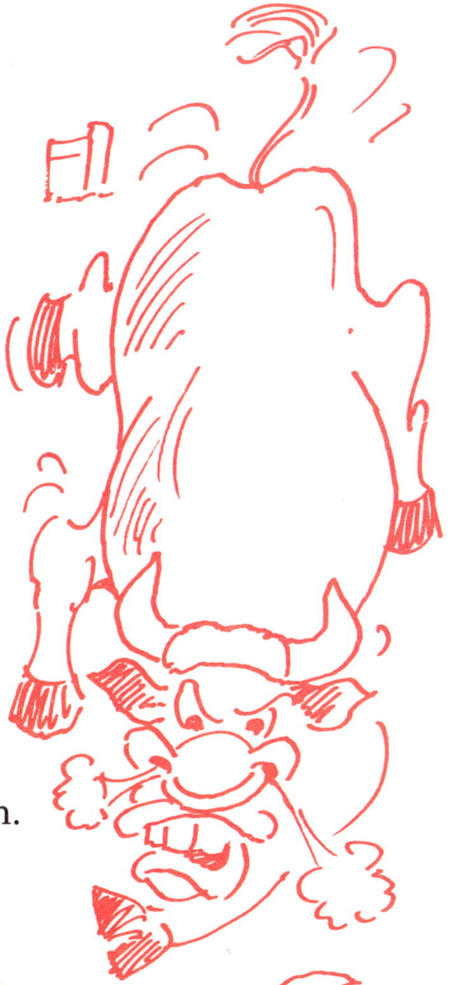

a The rose b _ _ _ has lots of flowers.
b Do you take s _ _ _ _ in your tea?
c Mike loves chocolate ice-cream for p _ _ _ _ _ _ .
d That b _ _ _ has long sharp horns.
e My bucket is f _ _ _ of water.
f Sophie has p _ _ _ _ _ out her loose tooth.
g P _ _ _ the button to start the game.

2 Use the words in the box to complete the sentences below. Write them in your book.

could **should** **would**

a Charlotte c _ _ _ _ not finish her work.
b W _ _ _ _ you like some sweets?
c You s _ _ _ _ _ wash your hands before meals.

Soft c

1 Use the words in the box to complete the sentences below. Write them in your book.

cell chance dance face fence prince since

a That clown had a funny f _ _ _ .

b A queen's son is called a p _ _ _ _ _ .

c Harnek had a c _ _ _ _ _ to play in the school team.

d The prisoner was put in a c _ _ _ .

e Jody loves to d _ _ _ _ to disco music.

f Dad put a f _ _ _ _ around our garden.

g I haven't seen auntie s _ _ _ _ Tuesday.

2 Use the clues and the words in the box to complete the words below. Write the words in your book.

cent centre lance pence pencil

a	the middle	c _ _ _ _ _
b	one hundred make a pound	p _ _ _ _
c	an American coin	c _ _ _
d	a weapon used long ago	l _ _ _ _
e	we use this to write	p _ _ _ _ _

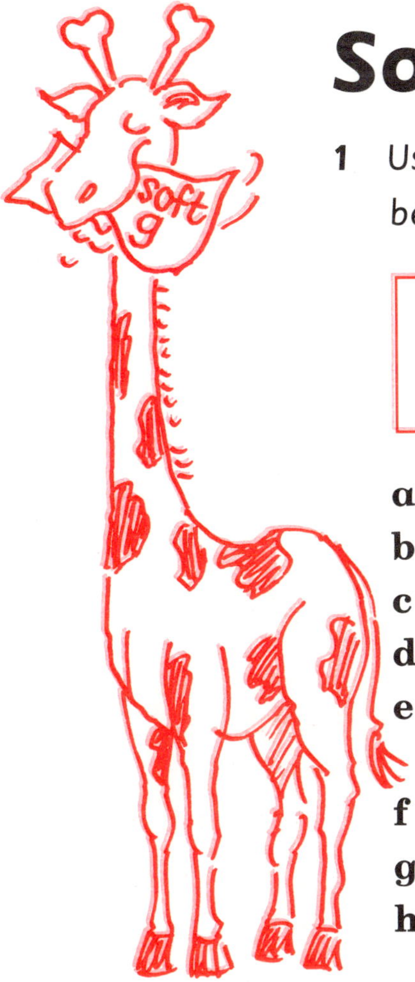

Soft g

1 Use the words in the box to complete the sentences below. Write them in your book.

gentle geography giant
giraffe huge large page stage

a The g _ r _ _ _ _ is the tallest animal on Earth .
b Look at p _ _ _ 24 in the book .
c The g _ _ _ _ chased Jack down the beanstalk.
d Sue was frightened of the h _ _ _ spider.
e We learnt about the weather in our g _ _ _ _ _ _ _ _ lesson at school.
f A mouse is small, but an elephant is l _ _ _ _ .
g You must be g _ _ _ _ _ with a tiny baby.
h The audience booed when the actor came on s _ _ _ _ .

2 Match each word below with the correct picture. Copy the words into your book.

a

b

c

d

barge **gem** **gentleman** **orange**

Silent k

knee kneel knight knit knock knot know

1 Use the words in the box to complete the sentences below.

a Sir Geoffrey is a brave k _ _ _ _ _ .
b Cathy could not untie the k _ _ _ in her laces.
c There was a loud k _ _ _ _ at the door.
d Do you k _ _ _ his name?
e Mrs Davies showed me how to k _ _ _ .
f The footballer cut his k _ _ _ .
g You must k _ _ _ _ before the queen.

Silent b

bomb climb crumb lamb thumb

2 Use the words in the box to complete the sentences below. Write them in your book.

a Uncle Jim had to c _ _ _ _ the tree.
b There was not a c _ _ _ _ of cake left.
c Mrs Allen put a plaster on Carl's sore t _ _ _ _ .
d The b _ _ _ exploded and hurt two people.
e The l _ _ _ was running across the field.

Silent h

ghost honest hour

3 Use the words in the box to complete the sentences below. Write them in your book.

a The g _ _ _ _ haunted the ruined castle.
b It took me an h _ _ _ to mow the lawn.
c Tony is always h _ _ _ _ _ and tells the truth.

ai

1 Use the words in the box to complete the sentences below. Write them in your book.

hail nail pail pain
sailed rain tail wail

a The mouse had a long t _ _ _ .
b The hungry baby gave a loud w _ _ _ .
c Martin had a p _ _ _ in his tummy.
d Everyone ran indoors out of the r _ _ _ .
e The window cleaner filled his p _ _ _ with water.
f Louise banged a n _ _ _ into the wood.
g The h _ _ _ rattled at the window.
h The boat s _ _ _ _ _ up the River Nile.

2 Use the words in the box to complete the sentences below. Write them in your book.

afraid curtains paint
snail train waiting

a Hannah got red p _ _ _ _ all over her blouse.
b Pull the c _ _ _ _ _ _ _ _, please.
c The s _ _ _ _ crept slowly along the path.
d Katie was a _ _ _ _ _ of the dark.
e Kulbir was w _ _ _ _ _ _ for his turn on the computer.
f Peter had a t _ _ _ _ set for his birthday.

Looking back

1 Use the words in the box to complete the sentences below. Write them in your book.

above	**April**	**brother**	**climb**
every	**knives**	**oil**	**pushed**
should	**tail**	**twice**	**voyage**

a Please put the k _ _ _ _ _ on the table.
b The caretaker put o _ _ on the squeaky door.
c You s _ _ _ _ _ never talk to strangers.
d The rocket went on a v _ _ _ _ _ into space.
e The month after March is A _ _ _ _ .
f A dog needs a walk e _ _ _ _ day.
g The opposite of below is a _ _ _ _ .
h The children ran round the field t _ _ _ _ .
i It is dangerous to c _ _ _ _ trees.
j Ann's b _ _ _ _ _ _ is two years older than she is.
k The baby pulled the cat's t _ _ _ .
l The bully p _ _ _ _ _ Helen off the swing.

ar

1 Choose the correct word from the box to complete the sentences below. Write them in your book.

arm	**car**	**dark**	**far**	**hard**	**mark**	**shark**

a The c _ _ came around the corner too fast.
b Mark slipped on the ice and broke his a _ _ .
c The singer had a big dirty m _ _ _ on his shirt.
d The butter was very h _ _ _ .
e The old man could not run very f _ _ .
f The owl came out when it was d _ _ _ .
g The s _ _ _ _ had huge, sharp teeth.

2 Use the words in the box to solve the puzzle. Write them in your book.

army	**farm**	**bark**	**cards**	**lark**	**tar**	**cart**

a	the noise a dog makes	b _ _ _
b	you get these on your birthday	c _ _ _ _
c	animals may live here	f _ _ _
d	you find this on the road	t _ _
e	a bird	l _ _ _
f	a lot of soldiers	a _ _ _
g	a horse may pull this	c _ _ _

aw

1 *Choose the eggs from the nest to complete the sentences below. Write them in your book.*

a The baby is learning to c _ _ _ l .
b Sam's cat has sharp c _ _ _ s .
c Lions like to eat r _ _ meat.
d The boxer had a broken j _ _ .
e The weather has been a _ _ _ _ this week.
f The Sun rises at d _ _ _ .
g The h _ _ _ hovered over the mouse.

2 *Use the words in the box to solve the clues. Write them in your book.*

draw	**law**	**lawn**	**paw**
prawn	**saw**	**straw**	**yawn**

a you do this when you are tired — y _ _ _
b this creature lives in the sea — p _ _ _ _
c a green grassy patch — l _ _ _
d a dog's foot — p _ _
e you can do this with a pencil — d _ _ _
f something you must not break — l _ _
g a tool for cutting wood — s _ _
h you drink through one of these — s _ _ _ _

be ack

1 Use the words in the box to complete the sentences below. Write them in your book.

because	**before**	**begin**	**behave**
behind	**belong**	**Beware**	

a The teacher told me to b _ _ _ _ _ myself.
b Those sweets b _ _ _ _ _ to me.
c Brush your teeth b _ _ _ _ _ you go to bed.
d The sign said 'B _ _ _ _ _ of the dog'.
e Listen carefully, b _ _ _ _ _ _ I will not say it again.
f If you are ready, we will b _ _ _ _ .
g Alice was hiding b _ _ _ _ _ the door.

2 Use the words in the box and the signs to decode the words below. Write them in your book.

back	**black**	**crack**
smack	**stack**	**track**

b △	**bl** ▭	**cr** ○
sm ▯	**st** ⊙	**tr** □

a △ ack **d** ⊙ ack
b ○ ack **e** □ ack
c ▯ ack **f** ▭ ack

cr

1 Use the **cr** on the crab to begin the words below. Write them in your book. Now use the words to complete the sentences.

_ _ ab

_ _ y

_ _ isps

_ _ ow

_ _ oss

_ _ awl

a Kenny loves salt and vinegar _ _ isps.

b The big black _ _ ow flew away.

c The nasty _ _ ab nipped my toe.

d Laura's baby sister can _ _ awl.

e Mum was _ _ oss when I broke the glass.

f Aaron fell down and began to _ _ y.

2 Complete the words to solve the clues. Write them in your book.

a the sound a frog makes _ _ oak

b a tiny piece of bread _ _ umb

c we pull these at Christmas _ _ ackers

d the noise when you eat crisps _ _ unch

e an accident between two cars _ _ ash

ea says e, ee and er

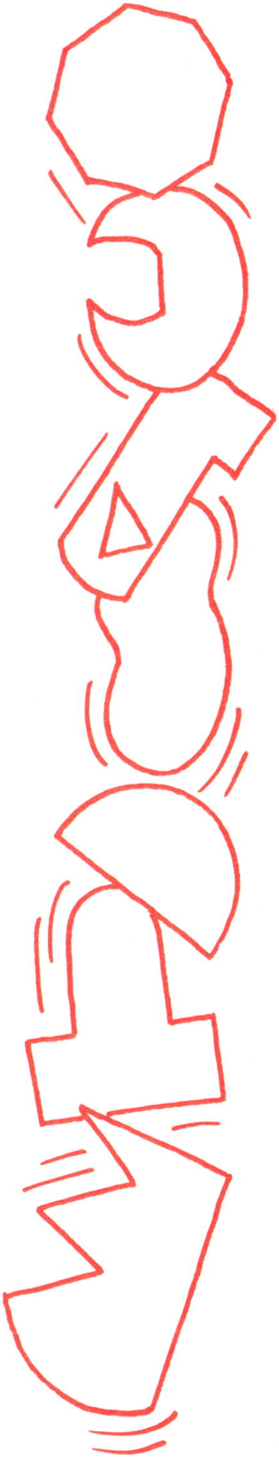

1 Use the shape clues to help you complete the sentences below. Write the sentences in your book.

bread **feather** **head** **read** **ready**

a Georgina fell and bumped her 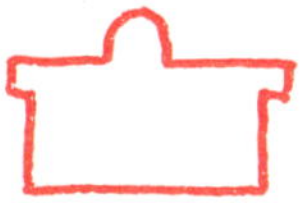

b Robin Hood had a 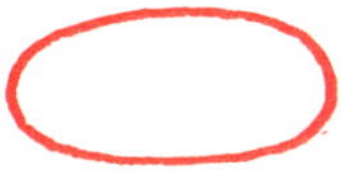 in his cap.

c Tom had  and jam for his tea.

d Are you  for school?

e Tanya has just  *The Secret Garden*.

2 Use the shape clues to find the missing words. Write the sentences in your book.

 **beans**  **meat**  **sea**

a Adam likes to paddle in the 

b Mum made a  pie for tea.

c Kate likes  on toast for tea.

3 Use the words in the box to complete the sentences below.

early	**learn**	**search**

a Sue always arrives at school e _ _ _ _ .

b Ruth wants to l _ _ _ _ to play the piano.

c Please help me s _ _ _ _ _ for my coat.

wh

1 Use the words in the box to complete the sentences below. Write them in your book.

whale wheat wheel
while whip whisper white

a The huge w _ _ _ _ swam around the ship.
b Adam made his clean w _ _ _ _ shirt dirty.
c The circus master cracked his w _ _ _ .
d The postman's bike had a broken w _ _ _ _ .
e Bread is made from w _ _ _ _ .
f It is rude to w _ _ _ _ _ _ .
g Wait here w _ _ _ _ I buy some sweets.

2 Use the words in the box to complete the sentences below. Write them in your book.

what when where which who whose

a Tell me _h_ your best friend is.
b I know w _ _ r _ you are going on holiday.
c Find out at _ _ a _ time the train leaves.
d Nobody knows _ _ _ _ h of these shirts is clean.
e I can guess w _ _ s _ trainers these are.
f Let us know _ _ _ n you can come to tea.

ew ey

1 The rain has washed away the **ew** from the words below. Use the words in the box to fill them in. Write them in your book.

chew few flew grew knew new news sew stew

a fl _ _ **b** kn _ _ **c** st _ _ **d** n _ _ **e** s _ _

2 Use the words in the box to complete the sentences below. Write them in your book.

a There were very f _ _ coins left in the money box.
b The sunflower g _ _ _ very tall.
c The cow loves to c _ _ _ the grass.
d Nicholas liked to watch the n _ _ _ .

3 Use the words in the box to complete the sentences below.

donkey honey key money monkey

a The m _ _ _ _ _ swung from tree to tree.
b Mum used her k _ _ to unlock the door.
c Pooh Bear loves h _ _ _ _ .
d I had a d _ _ _ _ _ ride on the beach.
e Joe spent all his pocket m _ _ _ _ on sweets.

ir

1 Use the words in the box to complete the sentences below. Write them in your book.

birthday circus dirty first shirt skirt stir

a The dog was very d _ _ _ _ after playing in the mud.

b Nicola has a new school s _ _ _ _ .

c I had lots of presents for my b _ _ _ _ _ _ _ .

d Uncle bought a new s _ _ _ _ at the shops.

e The c _ _ _ _ _ clowns were very funny.

f Peter came f _ _ _ _ in the sack race.

g Favida helped her sister to s _ _ _ the cake mix.

2 Complete the puzzle. Write the words in your book.

birthday fir first girl thirsty thirty

a the day you were born

b opposite of boy

c needing a drink

d a type of tree

e a number

f opposite of last

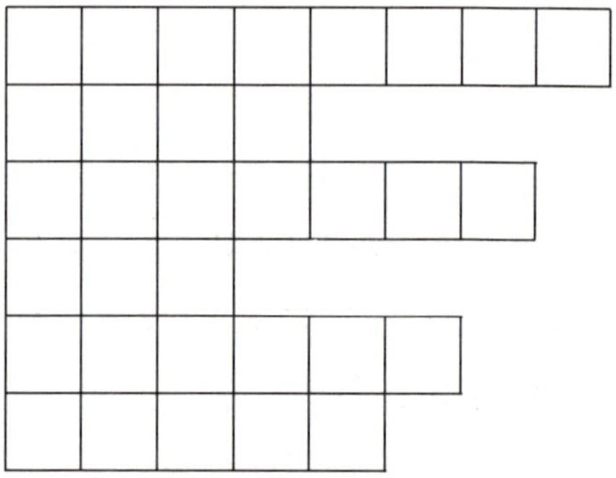

or

1 Help Roy the rhinoceros to put the words in the correct sentences. Write them in your book.

born doctor forget horn
more or story torn

a Would you like some m _ _ _ ice cream?
b The baby was b _ _ _ yesterday.
c When Mollie was ill, she went to see the d _ _ _ _ _ .
d Ranjit's trousers were t _ _ _ .
e Do you want an orange lolly _ _ a lemon one?
f Fiona wrote a very long s _ _ _ _ .
g The rhinoceros had a huge h _ _ _ .
h Don't f _ _ _ _ _ Julia's birthday.

2 Match the clues to the words on the signpost. Write them in your book.

a someone who visits
b meat of pigs
c acts on a stage
d a mistake
e add ten to thirty
f early part of the day

ou

1 Use the words in the box to complete the sentences below. Write them in your book.

count ground house pound proud south

a The child fell on the stony g _ _ _ _ _ .
b We are moving to a new h _ _ _ _ .
c Rachel was very p _ _ _ _ of her new doll.
d I c _ _ _ _ my pocket money carefully.
e Grandad gave me a shiny p _ _ _ _ coin.
f Chris went north but Robert went s _ _ _ _ .

2 Fit the words below into the word grid. Write them in your book.

cloud loud mouse mouth out round

a opposite of in
b small animal
c your tongue is in this
d very noisy
e found in the sky
f like a circle

ow

1 Fill in the missing words. Write the sentences in your book.

clown cow crowd How now town

a The c _ _ eats grass.
b Mum and Dad went shopping in the t _ _ _ .
c The c _ _ _ _ threw a custard pie.
d H _ _ are you feeling?
e The little boy got lost in the c _ _ _ _ .
f Joe has to go home n _ _ .

2 Find the correct word to complete the sentences below. Write them in your book.

blow low mow throw pillow snow window yellow

a Can you b _ _ _ up this balloon?
b It is cold enough for s _ _ _ to fall.
c Cows love to eat y _ _ _ _ _ buttercups.
d It is very dangerous to t _ _ _ _ stones.
e Claire likes a soft p _ _ _ _ _ to sleep on.
f David kicked the football and broke the w _ _ _ _ _ .
g The little stool was too l _ _ .
h I help my sister to m _ _ the lawn.

How wise are you?

1 Use the words in the box to complete the sentences below. Write them in your book.

art	**attack**	**below**	**crayons**	**eagle**	
Earth	**hawk**	**keys**	**leather**	**order**	**our**
owl	**swirl**	**threw**	**whistle**		

a The h _ _ _ swooped and caught the mouse.
b The pilot saw the runway b _ _ _ _ him.
c These shoes are made of l _ _ _ _ _ r.
d The referee blew his wh _ _ _ _ _ for half time.
e Rosie t _ _ _ w the ball on the roof.
f We painted a picture in the _ _ _ lesson.
g Beth used her c _ _ y _ _ _ to colour the picture.
h I watched the water s _ _ _ l down the drain.
i We ride _ _ _ bikes to school.
j The golden e _ g _ _ flew high in the air.
k The driver has lost his car k _ y _ .
l Put these numbers in the correct o _ _ e _ .
m We live on planet E _ _ _ h.
n The soldiers made an at _ _ _ _ on the enemy.
o The barn _ _ _ hunts for food at night.

tr

1 Choose the words to match the pictures. Copy the pictures and the words into your book.

a

b

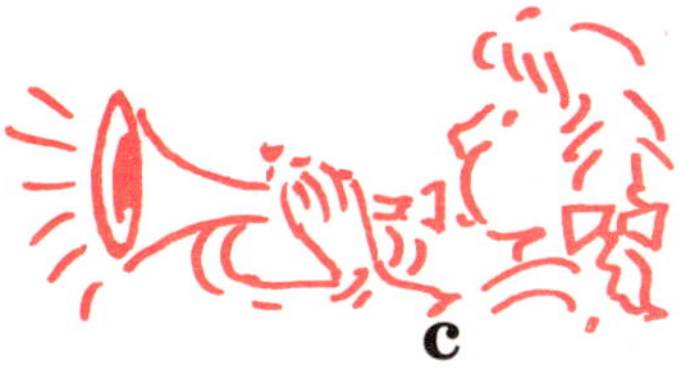

c

d

e

f

tractor **tray** **tree** **tricycle** **trolley** **trumpet**

2 Use the words in the box to complete the sentences below. Write them in your book.

train travel triangle trick
trousers true trunk try

a A t _ _ a _ _ _ _ has three sides.
b We missed the t _ _ _ n to London.
c The magician did a clever card t _ _ _ k .
d The elephant picked up leaves with its t _ u _ _ .
e Is it t _ _ _ that Sam has had an accident?
f I'll t _ _ to get all my spellings right.
g Alan has some new, grey t _ _ _ s _ _ _ .
h Mina wanted to t _ _ _ _ l the world.

Double consonants

1 Draw the pictures in your book and label them correctly.

a

b

c

d

e

f

balloon cherry glass letter squirrel rabbit

2 Choose an egg to complete the words below. Use the words to finish the sentences. Write them in your book.

rr ss

ff ll

mm tt pp

a The little girl was playing with her mu _ _ y.
b There is je _ _ y and ice-cream for pudding.
c James put too much bu _ _ er on his bread.
d We can't a _ _ ord a new car this year.
e Nobody enjoyed the swimming le _ _ on.
f The queen looked in the mi _ _ or.
g Cedric had an a _ _ le in his lunch box.

Word mix

1 Copy the pictures into your book. Use the words to label them correctly.

a 

c 

b 

d 

bridge children door police

2 Use the words in the box to complete the sentences below. Write them in your book.

able after doing friends once people pretty upon walk were

a There was a crowd of p _ _ _ _ _ at the market.
b We took the dog for a w _ _ _ along the canal.
c Kim was ill and not a _ _ _ to go to school.
d You must run o _ _ _ around the track.
e The girls went out to play a _ _ _ _ tea.
f They w _ _ _ just going out when the phone rang.
g My sister is d _ _ _ _ her homework.
h The pattern on the plate was very p _ _ _ _ _ .
i Once u _ _ _ a time there lived a dragon.
j The two boys are the best of f _ _ _ _ _ s.

How many?

1 Use the words in the box to complete the sentences below. Write them in your book.

centimetres grams hour kilogram kilometres litre metres miles millimetres minutes pints seconds

a The ant was two m ____________ long.
b Sarah bought a k ________ of sugar.
c The milkman leaves us three p ____ of milk a day.
d We have to walk two k __________ to school.
e It took Polly ten m ______ to eat her breakfast.
f My desk is 70 c ____________ wide.
g Dad put 200 g ____ of flour in the cake.
h We have only an h ___ to eat our lunch.
i I bought one l ____ of orange juice.
j A minute is 60 s ______ .
k The classroom door is two m _____ high.
l We live 50 m ____ from London.

More than one

Plural means **more than one**.

Some words that end in **y** change to plural by changing the **y** into **ies**.

a bab**y**  two bab**ies** 

a lorr**y**  three lorr**ies** 

1 Use the words in the box to correct the sentences below. Write them in your book.

cherries	**flies**	**ladies**	**lollies**	**poppies**

a Kim bought a bag of **cherry** .
b Two **lady** sat chattering on the bench.
c I picked a bunch of **poppy** .
d Paul likes strawberry **lolly** best.
e There were hundreds of **fly** around the bin.

Some words that end in ***f*** change to plural by changing the ***f*** into **ves**.

a lea***f*** lea**ves**

2 Use the words in the box to correct the sentences below. Write them in your book.

hooves	**knives**	**wolves**

a Ben put the **knife** and forks on the table.
b The horses' **hoof** made a clattering sound.
c The **wolf** howled on the cold night.

Words that sound the same

pair  **pear** 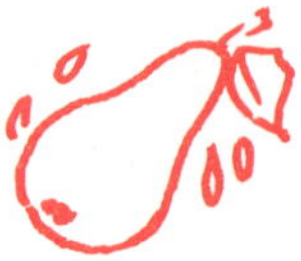

hare  **hair** 

1 Choose the correct words to complete each pair of sentences below.

a William looks very p___ today. — **pail**
b The farmer filled her p___ with water. — **pale**

c You need eggs, sugar, f____ and fat to make a cake. — **flour**
d That pink rose is a lovely f_____. — **flower**

e Alison can w____ very neatly. — **write**
f All her work was r____. — **right**

g Put the plate over t____ please. — **their**
h They lost t____ ball in the park. — **there**

i Please be ready to go in an ____. — **our**
j We put ___ coats in the cupboard. — **hour**

2 Look at the pairs of words below. Use a dictionary to find the meaning of each word. Write it in your book.

a soar
sore

b fur
fir

c leek
leak

d there
their

e bear
bare

st tch

1 Use the words in the box to complete the sentences below.

fast	stamp	stool	stop	twist

a Terry is a very f _ _ _ runner.
b Gran stuck a s _ _ _ _ on the envelope.
c You have to s _ _ _ at a red traffic light.
d To open the jar, t _ _ _ _ the lid.
e Jack fell off the high s _ _ _ _ .

2 Use the words in the box to complete the sentences below.

catch	hatch	switch	Watch

a Press the s _ _ _ _ _ to start the engine.
b We saw the chick h _ _ _ _ from the egg.
c W _ _ _ _ me, then see if you can do it too.
d Tim could not c _ _ _ _ the ball.

3 Stella the starfish invented this code.

a = 1	b = 2	c = 3	d = 4	e = 5	f = 6
g = 7	h = 8	i = 9	j = 10	k = 11	and up to z = 26

Write out the code and use it to work out the **st** and **tch** words below. Write the words in your book.

a 19 : 9 : 19 : 20 : 5 : 18
b 9 : 20 : 3 : 8
c 19 : 3 : 18 : 1 : 20 : 3 : 8
d 13 : 15 : 19 : 20
e 13 : 1 : 20 : 3 : 8
f 19 : 20 : 9 : 3 : 11

qu squ

1 Use the words in the box to complete the sentences below. Write them in your book.

quack quarrel quiet quiz square squid

a The girls had a q _ _ _ _ _ _ over some sweets.

b A s _ _ _ _ lives in the sea.

c The children were very q _ _ _ _ when the teacher read the story.

d All of us tried very hard in the maths q _ _ _ .

e The duck gave a loud q _ _ _ _ .

f The summer fete is held in the village s _ _ _ _ _ .

2 Choose **squ** or **qu** to complete the words below. Use the words to complete the sentences.

een estions irrel eue antity ash

a The cook measured the correct _ _ antity of flour.

b There were some very difficult _ _ estions in the history test.

c The _ _ een had a golden coach.

d The children like to drink orange _ _ _ ash.

e The _ _ _ irrel eats nuts.

f The _ _ eue for the bus was very long.

Tiger time

1 Use the words in the box to complete the sentences below. Write them in your book.

for	**four**	**friends**	**hospital**	**leaves**
lorry	**match**	**minutes**	**parties**	**quick**
stars	**tomorrow**	**traffic**	**trip**	**walks**

a There was lots of t _ _ ff _ _ on the busy street.
b Ahmed w _ _ k _ to school each day.
c Sophie got a bike f _ r her birthday.
d Hannah invited three f _ _ _ n _ _ to tea.
e Tie your shoelaces or you will t _ _ p up.
f Next week Joanna is going to three p _ _ t _ _ _ .
g The fallen l _ _ v _ _ covered the ground.
h The big l _ _ _ y stopped at the traffic lights.
i Be q _ _ c _ or you will miss the train.
j Dad had f _ _ r sandwiches for lunch.
k There are 30 m _ _ u _ _ _ in half an hour.
l Simon is going to the dentist to _ _ _ _ _ _ _ .
m The st _ _ _ shone brightly in the dark night.
n Adrian broke his leg and went to the h _ _ p _ _ _ _ .
o Ben and Sarah went to the football m _ _ _ h.

Adding ing to doing words

1 Copy the grid into your book and complete it.
The first word has been done for you.

hop	**hopping**
skip	s
clap	c
run	r
knit	k
drip	d
slip	s
drop	d
sit	s
stop	s

2 Did you remember to double
the last letter before adding **ing**?
Complete the words in **bold**.
Write the sentences in your book.

a The baker was **hum** a tune.
b The pony was **trot** to the stable.
c The baby was **begin** to cry.
d Uncle was **rub** his sore elbow.
e The bathroom tap was **drip**.
f Emma is going **shop** tomorrow.
g The sparrow was **flap** its wings.
h Who was **cut** the hedge?
i Shiri was **dab** the cut on her finger.
j The lorry was **tip** rubbish at the dump.

ice age

1 Use the words in the box to complete the sentences below. Write them in your book.

ice	**mice**	**price**	**rice**	**slice**	**spice**	**twice**

a The m _ _ _ nibbled at the cheese.
b Paul has been to France t _ _ _ _ .
c Would you like a s _ _ _ _ of apple pie?
d What is the p _ _ _ _ of this book?
e Donna loves to go i _ _ skating.
f Tom added cherries and s _ _ _ _ to the cake.
g Rob's favourite meal is chicken with fried r _ _ _ .

2 Use the words in the box to complete the sentences below. Write them in your book.

age	**bandage**	**garage**	**page**
stage	**sausage**	**voyage**	

a The nurse put a b _ _ _ _ _ _ on David's knee.
b Dad had to take the car to the g _ _ _ _ _ .
c Alex started reading the wrong p _ _ _ .
d The ship went on a long v _ _ _ _ _ .
e The actor ran on to the s _ _ _ _ .
f Ted loves s _ _ _ _ _ _ and chips.
g Write your name and a _ _ on the form.

any every some no

1 Place each word below in the right list.
Write the lists in your book.

everybody anything someone nothing
anybody somehow nobody something
somebody everything everyone

no	any	some	every
nobody	anything	something	everybody

2 Look at Harry's code.

___ any ___ no ___ some ___ every

Use the code to complete the sentences below.
Write them in your book. Check your spellings with the words at the top of the page.

a I knocked, but ___ body came to the door.

b Nearly ___ one wanted orange to drink.

c The doctor said there was ___ thing wrong with my knee.

d I think ___ body has eaten all the chocolate!

e Martin will get to the match ___ how.

f I'm afraid I can't do ___ thing to help you.

Adjectives to nouns

1 Boris the bloodhound has a special code.
Use his code to find the words below.
Write them in your book.

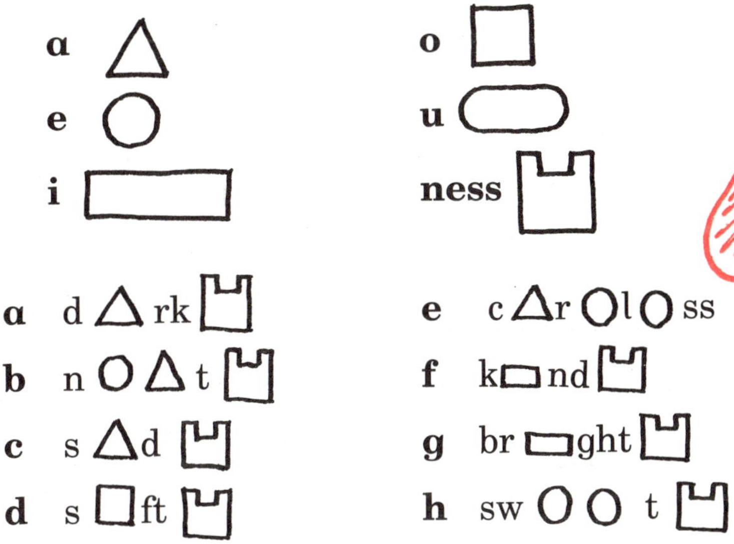

2 Use the words to complete the sentences below.

a The boy's work was wrong due to his c ____________.

b Claire got a star for the n ________ of her work.

c Kirsty showed her k ________ by sharing her sweets.

d There was great s _______ when the dog died.

e The owl liked to hunt in the d ________.

f The dog liked the s _________ of the chocolate.

g Amy loved the s ________ of her new pillow.

h The b ___________ of the light hurt the baby's eyes.

Break for lunch

1 Use the words in the box to complete the sentences below. Write them in your book.

afternoon break enjoys lose talk wonderful

a We will go out this a _ _ _ _ _ _ _ _ .

b Be careful, don't l _ _ _ your pocket money.

c Grandad always e _ _ _ _ _ a Chinese meal.

d If you drop that cup it will b _ _ _ _ .

e Rachel had a w _ _ _ _ _ _ _ _ day at the zoo.

f Be silent and do not t _ _ _ .

2 Use the words in the box to complete the puzzle. Write them in your book.

breakfast buy floor poor remember wild

a opposite of forget

b first meal of the day

c not tame

d you walk on this

e opposite of sell

f not rich

r _ _ _ _ _ _ _
b _ _ _ _ _ _ _ _
w _ _ _
f _ _ _ _
b _ _
p _ _ _

At the shops

1 Use the words in the box to complete the sentences below.
Write them in your book.

assistants baker basket butcher checkout chemist customers greengrocer newsagent supermarket till trolley

a On Fridays, we go shopping in the s _ _ _ _ _ _ _ _ _ _ _ .

b The n _ _ _ _ _ _ _ t sells newspapers and sweets.

c People who work in shops are called shop a _ _ _ _ _ _ _ _ s.

d Meat is sold by a b _ _ _ _ _ _ .

e Dad put all the shopping in a t _ _ _ _ _ y.

f You pay for your shopping at the c _ _ _ _ _ _ t.

g The money is put into the t _ _ l.

h Gran went to the g _ _ _ _ _ _ _ _ _ r to buy her vegetables.

i The c _ _ _ _ _ t sells plasters and medicines.

j I saw you buying bread and cakes at the b _ _ _ _ ' s shop.

k The shops were crowded with c _ _ _ _ _ _ _ s.

l Sarah carried her shopping in her b _ _ _ _ t.

Water

1 Use the words in the box to complete the sentences below. Write them in your book.

clouds	**oceans**	**rain**	**water cycle**

a Water in rivers and o _ _ _ _ _ evaporates.

b Water is held in the sky in c _ _ _ _ _ _ .

c When clouds become too heavy, the water falls as r _ _ _ .

d This is called the w _ _ _ _ c _ _ _ _ _ .

2 Use the clues on the hippo to help complete the grid. Write the words in your book.

ice **floats** **puddles** **sink** **steam** **river**

a frozen water

b opposite of sinks

c flows to the sea

d opposite of float

e boiling water gives off _ _ _ _ _ _ .

f children splash through these after it has rained

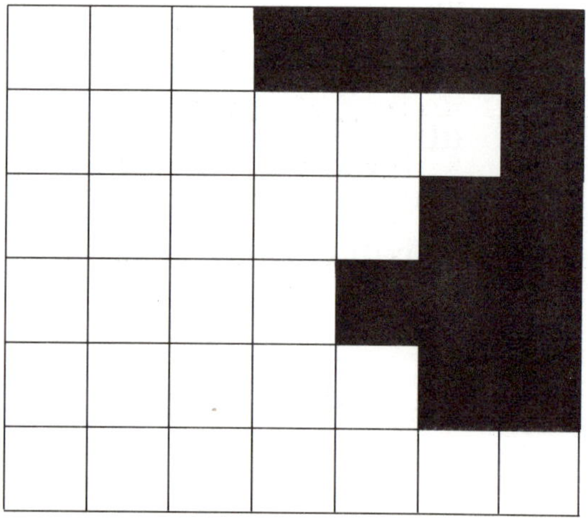

Roman invaders

1 Use the words in the box to complete the sentences below. Write them in your book.

Celts	**gladiators**	**Hadrian's Wall**	
javelins	**Julius Caesar**	**legions**	**shields**
swords	**toga**	**villa**	**woad**

a About 2000 years ago, the people who lived in Britain were called C _ _ t _ .

b J _ _ _ _ s C _ _ _ _ _ invaded Britain in 55 BC.

c The Celts painted themselves blue with w _ _ _ to frighten the Romans.

d The Romans and Celts fought with ja _ _ _ _ _ _ and sw _ _ _ _ .

e They used sh _ _ _ _ _ to protect themselves.

f Roman men wore a robe called a t _ _ _ .

g The Roman army was divided into l _ g _ _ _ _ .

h In the arena there were fights between gl _ _ _ _ t _ _ _ .

i H _ d _ _ _ _ _ W _ _ _ was built to protect Roman Britain from the Picts.

j A Roman house was called a v _ _ _ a .

2 Draw these pictures. Write the names to go with them in your book.

a sw _ _ d

b s _ _ _ ld

c jav _ _ _ _

d glad _ _ _ _ _

Europe

London
Madrid
Oslo
Berlin
Rome
Paris
Athens
Brussels

1 *Unscramble the letters in* **bold** *and match the capital city to the country. Write them in your book.*

a Spain	**Mdriad**	**e** Italy	**Rmoe**
b France	**Prisa**	**f** Belgium	**Belussres**
c Germany	**Belinr**	**g** Norway	**Oosl**
d Greece	**Aenhst**	**h** Britain	**Ldnoon**

2 *Match the countries with the people. Write them in your book.*

a France	Italian
b Greece	British
c Italy	Norwegian
d Belgium	French
e Britain	Greek
f Norway	Belgian

Words for art

1 Copy the pictures into your book.
Put the correct word under each picture.

palette
brush
overall
easel
scissors

2 Choose the correct word from the palette to complete the sentences below. Write them in your book.

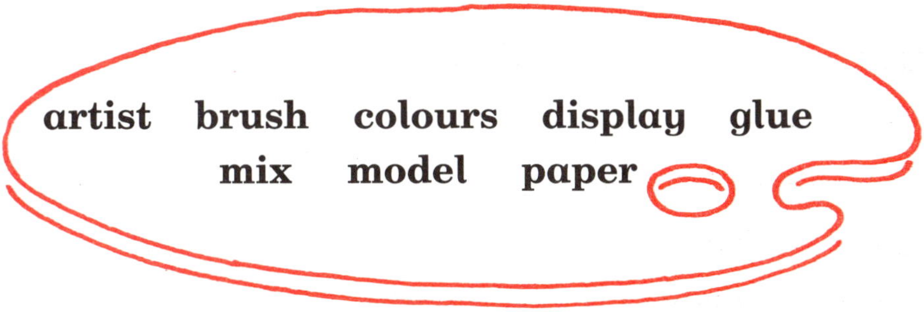

- **a** Helen dipped her b _ _ _ _ into the paint.
- **b** To make orange you m _ _ red and yellow.
- **c** The teacher used g _ _ _ to stick paper on to the card.
- **d** Simon was very pleased when his m _ _ _ _ was finished.
- **e** The artist's picture was full of bright c _ _ _ _ _ _ .
- **f** The children's work was on d _ _ _ _ _ _ in the hall.
- **g** The a _ _ _ _ _ painted a picture of the queen.
- **h** Shagusta pinned her p _ _ _ _ on the easel.

Last lap

1 *Use the words in the box to complete the sentences below. Write them in your book.*

after	**apple**	**behind**	**clapped**		
could	**floor**	**full**	**knit**	**litre**	**metres**
mother	**noisy**	**orange**	**pages**	**Rome**	
September	**supermarket**	**twitched**			

a The toddler hid the present b _ _ _ _ _ her back.
b The running track was thirty m _ _ _ _ _ long.
c R _ _ _ is the capital city of Italy.
d The a _ _ _ _ was ripe and rosy.
e Harry's story was three p _ _ _ _ long.
f Carla is going to play with the baby a _ _ _ _ school.
g Dad bought a three l _ _ _ _ bottle of orange for the party.
h The new term begins in S _ _ _ _ _ _ _ _ .
i Every week we go shopping at the s _ _ _ _ _ _ _ _ _ _ .
j My grandma showed me how to k _ _ _ .
k The angry cat t _ _ _ _ _ _ _ its tail.
l The litter bin was f _ _ _ of rubbish.
m The boy c _ _ _ _ not find his school bag.
n Everyone had a glass of o _ _ _ _ _ squash.
o The crowd c _ _ _ _ _ _ the winner of the race.
p The pups climbed all over their m _ _ _ _ _ .
q Karl spilt his tea all over the f _ _ _ _ .
r Concorde is very n _ _ _ _ as it takes off.

Word list

able
above
act
actor
afford
afraid
after
afternoon
age
alphabet
ant
antelope
anybody
anything
apple
April
arm
army
art
artist
assistants
Athens
atlas
attack
attic
August
awake
awful

babies
baby
back
baker
bakers
balloon
bandage
bare
barge
bark
basket
beans
bear
because
before
begin
beginning
behave
behind
Belgian
Belgium
bell
belong
below
Berlin
beware
bill
birthday
black
blow
boil
bomb
bone
born
box
bread
break
breakfast
bridge
brightness
Britain
British
brother
brush
Brussels
bulb
bull
bush
butcher
butter
buy

cabbage
Caesar
car
card
cards
carelessness
cart
catch
ceiling
cell
Celts
cent
centimetres
centre
chair
chance
checkout
chemist
cherries
cherry
chew
children
Christmas
circus
clap
clapping
claw
climb
clock
cloud
clown
colours
come
could
count
cow
crab
crack
cracker
crackers
crash
crawl
crayons
crisps
croak
cross
crow
crowd
crumb
crunch
cry
curtains
customers
cutting
cycle

dabbing
damage
dance
dark
darkness
dawn
December
dirty
display
doctor
doing
done
donkey
door
draw
drinking
drip
dripping
drop
dropping
drown

eagle
early
earth
easel
edge
egg
elbow
elephant
empty
enjoys
error
ever
every
everybody
everyone
everything

face
far
farm
fast
fastest
feather
February
fence
few
fir
first
flapping
flew
flies
floats
floor
flour
flower
for
forget
forty
four
France
French
friend
friends
full
fur

garage
gem
gentle
gentleman
geography
ghost
giant
giraffe
girl
gladiators
glass
glove
glue
grams
Greece
Greek
greengrocer
grew
ground

Hadrian's
hail
hair
hard
hatch
hare
hawk
head
holly
honest
honey
hooves
hop
hopping
horn
horse
hospital
hour
house
how
huge
humming

ice
Italian
Italy

January
javelins
jaw
jelly
Julius
July
June

kangaroo
key
keys
kilogram
kilometres
kindness
knee
kneel
knew
knight
knit
knitting
knives
knock
knot
know

ladies
lamb
lance
large
lark
law
lawn
leaf
leak
learn
leather
leaves
leek
legions
lesson
letter
litre
lollies
London
lorries
lorry
lose
loud
low

Madrid
March
mark
match
May
meat
message
metres
mice
miles
millimetres
minute
minutes
mirror
mix
model
money
monkey
more
morning
mother
mouse
mouth
mow
Mummy

nail
neatness
new
news
newsagent
nobody
noisy
north
Norway
Norwegian
nothing
November
now

oceans
October
oil
once
or
orange
order
Oslo
our
out
oven
overall
owl

page
pages
pail
pain
paint
pair
pale
palette
paper
Paris
parties
paw
pear
pence
pencil
people
pillow
pint
pints
police
poor
poppies
pork
pound
prawn
pretty
price
prince
proud
pudding
puddles
pulled
push
pushed

quack
quantity
quarrel
queen
questions
queue
quick
quiet
quiz

rabbit
rage
rain
raw
read
ready
red
remember
rice
right
river
Rome
room
round
rubbing
run
running

sadness
sail
sailed
sausage
saw
scissors
sea
seal
search
seconds
September
sew
shark
shields
shirt
shopping
should
since
sitting
sink
sit
skip
skipping
skirt
sleep
slice
slip
slipping
smack
snail
snake
snow
soar
softness
soil
soldiers
somebody
somehow
someone
something
son
sore
south
space
Spain
spice
spoil
square
squash
squid
squirrel
stack
stage
stamp
stars
stay
steam
stew
stir
stool
stop
stopping
story
straw
stream
sugar
supermarket
sweetness
swirl
switch
swords

tail
talk
tar
teacher
their
there
thieves
thirsty
thirty
threw
throw
thumb
till
tipping
toga
tomorrow
torn
town
track
tractor
traffic
train
travel
tray
tree
triangle
trick
tricycle
trip
trolley
trombone
trotting
trousers
true
trumpet
trunk
try
twice
twist
twitched

upon

villa
visitor
voice
voyage

wail
waiting
walk
walks
wall
watch
water
were
whale
what
wheat
wheel
when
where
which
while
whip
whisper
whistle
white
who
whose
why
wild
window
woad
wolves
won
wonderful
would
write

yawn
yellow